HUDSON AUTOMOBILES

1934-1957 PHOTO ARCHIVE

Byron D. Olsen

Iconografix
Photo Archive Series

Iconografix
1830A Hanley Road
Hudson, Wisconsin 54016 USA

Library of Congress Control Number: 2003115054

ISBN 1-58388-110-7

Reprinted November 2012

Printed in The United States of America

Copyediting by Jane Mausser

Cover photo- see page 80

BOOK PROPOSALS

Iconografix is a publishing company specializing in books for transportation enthusiasts. We publish in a number of different areas, including Automobiles, Auto Racing, Buses, Construction Equipment, Emergency Equipment, Farming Equipment, Railroads & Trucks. The Iconografix imprint is constantly growing and expanding into new subject areas.

Authors, editors, and knowledgeable enthusiasts in the field of transportation history are invited to contact the Editorial Department at Iconografix, 1830A Hanley Road, Hudson, WI 54016.

Dedication

The author would like to dedicate this book and express considerable thanks and commendation to one of the foremost saviors of automotive history from within the industry itself, John Conde of Bloomfield Hills, Michigan. John worked many years in the Public Relations Department of Nash and later American Motors, and became the unofficial historian of these companies and their predecessors, including Hudson. He has written a number of books and articles on automotive history. Of equal importantance, John has been instrumental in saving thousands of pages of auto industry corporate records and photos that might otherwise have been thrown away. As a long time member of the Society of Automotive Historians and a Trustee of the National Automotive History Collection, John Conde has probably done more than all but a few to capture and preserve the documentation of the history of the American automobile.

Acknowledgments

Most of the photographs in this book are originally from the company files of the Hudson Motor Car Co., and are presented through the cooperation and generosity of the National Automotive History Collection (NAHC) of the Detroit Public Library, Detroit, Michigan. The author would like to express his special thanks to the NAHC and Mark Patrick, Curator, for sharing these pieces of automobile history and helping to make this book possible.

Other sources of information include:

The Cars That Hudson Built
John A. Conde
Arnold-Porter Publishing Company (1980)

Hudson: The Postwar Years
Richard M. Langworth
Motorbooks International (1977)

The American Motors Family Album
John A. Conde
American Motors Corporation (1976)

Standard Catalog of American Cars 1805–1942
Beverly Rae Kimes and Henry Austin Clark, Jr.
Krause Publications (First Edition, 1985)

Standard Catalog of American Cars 1946–1975
John Gunnell, Editor
Krause Publications (Third Edition, 1991)

Special Interest Autos magazine, various issues

Collectible Automobile magazine, various issues

Hudson Sales Catalogs, 1934–1957
Hudson Motor Car Company (author's collection)

"The Mighty Hornet: An Appreciation"
Bruce L. Mori-Kubo
The Milestone Car (Spring 1974)

"The Fabulous Hudson"
Tom McCahill, Tom Rhodes, and others
The Milestone Car (Autumn 1976)

The Production Figure Book for U.S. Cars
Jerry Heasley
Motorbooks International (1977)

"Hudson" (several articles)
Maurice D. Hendry, Robert F. Andrews, Don Vorderman, and others
Automobile Quarterly, Summer, 1971 (Vol. IX, No. 4)

Ownership
I owned three step-downs, a Hornet, and two convertibles.

Introduction

The Hudson Motor Car Company was organized in February 1909 in Detroit, which was already becoming the center of the exploding new automobile industry. The company name came from J. L. Hudson, the owner of Detroit's most prestigious department store and who provided some startup capital. However, the real founders were four men who already had experience in the industry: Roy Chapin, Howard Coffin, Roscoe Jackson, and George Dunham. All four had started with the Olds Motor Works, and Chapin and Coffin had experience with other car builders as well.

The new company quickly became a major player in the mushrooming automobile industry. Hudson established a strong sales growth record that continued through the 1920s. By 1916, Hudson production exceeded 25,000 cars for the year, a blazing start for a new manufacturer. Factors in Hudson growth after that included the Super Six engine introduced in 1916, and aggressive promoting of low cost closed bodies as exemplified by the 1922 Essex coach. At $1,495, it was the lowest priced sedan on the market. By 1929, Hudson sold 300,000 cars and actually reached third place in sales in the American automobile industry, ahead of every other car company except Ford and Chevrolet. This was an unprecedented achievement for a so-called "independent" manufacturer. "Independent" meant not affiliated with one of the big three: GM, Ford, or Chrysler.

The Great Depression struck with full force after 1929, and Hudson never again achieved the sales levels of the 1920s. That was not due to any lack of interesting products, as we shall see in the pages ahead. Guiding Hudson through the company's later years were Stuart Baits, engineering vice president; Frank Spring, the colorful head of the styling department; and A. E. Barit, who became president in 1936 after the untimely death of founder Roy Chapin. Together they fashioned some of the most interesting automobiles to come out of Detroit, often with limited resources.

Right from the beginning, Hudson emphasized performance when promoting its cars. That continued to the very end of Hudson's existence as an independent company. As early as 1916, Ralph Mulford drove a new Super Six to a stock car straightaway record of 102.5 miles per hour. That willingness to test Hudson cars at top speed and endurance events continued even during the 1930s, when most other car builders had backed away from such challenges and the potential embarrassment of failure. Performance challenges in the 1930s and 1940s consisted mostly of closed course single car speed and endurance record attempts, at which Hudson usually did well. By the 1940s, Hudson had developed a reputation as a fast car, probably because of its willingness to enter speed trials.

Hudson's finest hour as a performance car came near the end of its history. In 1951, the Hudson Hornet Six became almost unbeatable on America's stock car racetracks. The Hornet's powerful new engine, combined with the low center of gravity provided by the revolutionary step-down body, was further benefited by the excellent suspension and steering Hudson had used for years. Those were the days when the racecars were truly stock and could be bought off the showroom floor and raced. To enhance its leadership position, Hudson developed a variety of performance and handling components that could be factory installed on any new Hudson, even if the buyer did not intend to go racing.

The result was a most remarkable string of victories in stock car racing events from 1951 through 1954. Starting with Marshall Teague's first win in a Hornet February 11, 1951, Hudson amassed an amazing 124 first place finishes in major league stock car races through July 10, 1954. In many of these races, the second, third, and fourth place finishers were also Hudsons. By 1954, virtually all of the competitive cars were powered by modern overhead-valve short-stroke V-8 engines, often with large displacement. Yet, the rugged and simple Hornet inline flathead-six continued to take more than its share of victories. It was truly Hudson's finest hour, because these were not single car closed course timed speed trials. This was the rough and tumble of racetrack competition—wheel to wheel with the best that Detroit could muster.

Unfortunately, racing success did not translate into sufficient sales to keep the company healthy and provide funds to design and tool new products. What money Hudson had for product development was squandered on the Jet, which turned out to be an unpopular design in a car market segment that would not prosper until several years later. Nevertheless, Hudson left a legacy of design innovations that will be long remembered. Such features included center point steering, anti-sway and anti-roll bars, splayed rear leaf springs, oil bath clutches, dual-safe brakes, pre-selector and semi-automatic shifting, all steel bodies, and rugged unit construction bodies with recessed floors for a low center of gravity. Perhaps most important of all, the company showed a fearless willingness to compete against the best the competition could present, on the racetrack as well as on the street and highways.

Byron Olsen
St. Paul, Minnesota
May 2003

Hudson entered the streamlined era with its completely redesigned 1934 models. The grille and windshield were slanted back, and fenders were much more rounded with deeper skirts. This is a DeLuxe Eight sedan with 113 horsepower.

The new streamlined style was evident at the rear as well. For the first time on a Hudson sedan, the rear of the body tapered back instead of curving forward under the rear seat. The new shape permitted a built-in trunk compartment, which Hudson called a "luggage vestibule." Taillights on this 1934 DeLuxe Eight sedan were chrome plated and molded to the fender contour.

Spring is in the air and this gent has the top down even though the leaves are barely out yet. This is a Hudson DeLuxe Eight Convertible Coupe on a 116-inch wheelbase. All two-doors used this wheelbase, while some four-door sedan models were built on a 123-inch wheelbase.

This is a 1934 DeLuxe Eight Coupe, available with or without a rumble seat. The 254-cubic-inch L-head straight-eight engine powered all 1934 Hudsons; six-cylinder engines were relegated to the Terraplane line, which was sold as a separate marque.

Hudson introduced this trunk-back sedan model in 1934 that offered more luggage capacity than the flat-back model. Another option was a split front axle semi-independent front suspension called "Axleflex." It found few takers.

The Great Depression had not let up much, so in June 1934 Hudson introduced a lower priced, stripped down model on the 116-inch wheelbase called the Challenger. As seen here, one windshield wiper, fewer hood louvers, and chrome horns were a few of the deletions. Hudson shipped 27,130 cars plus another 56,804 Terraplanes for 1934—not bad considering the difficult economy.

For 1935, the streamlining was refined with new grilles and trim. This is a Hudson DeLuxe Eight with optional fender skirts and fender-mounted spare wheel. As on many cars in the mid-1930s, doors were hinged at the rear and opened to catch the wind, giving rise to the nickname "suicide doors."

Hudson advertised all-steel bodies for 1935, an industry first. Even the roof insert, which was fabric on other marques, was steel on Hudsons as can be seen on this Special Eight sedan being admired by executives and one engineer. Like the DeLuxe Eight, the lower priced Special Eight rode on a 117-inch wheelbase.

This is a Hudson Special Eight Touring Brougham. "Touring" meant a trunk back, and "Brougham" was Hudson's name for two-door sedans. The women were demonstrating the latest in beachwear for 1935.

Lots of Hudsons and Terraplanes were displayed at the 34th Annual Philadelphia Auto Show. The date was January 19, 1935, and several other marques can be glimpsed in the background on the lower exhibition floor of the Philadelphia Convention Hall. Hudson shipped 29,476 cars in 1935, plus 70,323 Terraplanes, up slightly from 1934.

Shown here is a trunk back, or "Touring" model four-door sedan, with extra cost side-mounted spare wheel and fender skirts. All Hudson eight-cylinder engines in 1935 were 254 cubic inches and developed 113 horsepower with 124 horsepower optional.

Coupes were available as two- or four-passenger models by means of an optional rumble seat, in which case the third and fourth passengers rode outside. This is a Special Eight Coupe. Another trailblazing new option for Hudson's 1935 models was the Electric Hand, an electric and vacuum powered pre-selector gearshift. Developed with Bendix Corporation, the shift lever was replaced with a small steering column-mounted "H" pattern switch used to select each gear. After moving the gear selector switch, the shift did not occur until the clutch was momentarily depressed.

Hudson was one of the few car builders in the 1930s to aggressively compete for performance records. This 1935 Special Eight set 36 AAA speed and endurance records at Muroc Dry Lake in California in April of 1935. Two of the records set were 93.03 miles per hour for 5 miles and 85.8 miles per hour for 1,000 miles. One of the drivers was Wilbur Shaw, a famous Indianapolis Speedway driver and later president of the Speedway.

For 1935, six-cylinder engines once again became available in the Hudson line along with the Terraplane sixes. Taking delivery of this snappy looking Hudson Big Six Convertible Coupe in Detroit on February 27, 1935 was film star Patricia Ellis. Judging by the date and the snow on the ground, it was a bit early for top down driving. The engine was a 212-cubic-inch L-head in-line six developing 93 horsepower with a 100-horsepower version available.

Hudson's finest for 1935 was the Custom Eight line on a 124-inch wheelbase. This car being displayed on a carpeted turntable was called the Brougham model because it had no rear quarter windows. The closed-in rear compartment that resulted, together with fender skirts and fender-mounted spare wheels, produced a very elegant limousine.

For 1936, Hudson was completely restyled with entirely new bodies, as well as an unusual new grille design. A new front suspension was introduced called Radial Safety Control. It used a solid front axle braced with two pivot arms to locate the axle more securely than with leaf springs alone.

The new body design was more rounded, as were the fenders. Interiors were much roomier and the front seat was 55 inches wide—room enough for three people. Most models, whether six or eight, used the same 120-inch wheelbase. This is a 1936 Hudson Custom Eight Brougham. The Terraplane was continued as a separate marque using the Hudson bodies, all powered by six-cylinder engines. Total Hudson sales for 1936 were 25,409 Hudsons and 93,309 Terraplanes.

Here is another Brougham, this one a DeLuxe Six. It is a Touring Brougham because it has a trunk back instead of a flat trunk lid. Hudson adopted hydraulic brakes in 1936, and added a unique feature that it would retain until the end of Hudson production in 1957. If hydraulic pressure ever failed, pushing further on the foot brake mechanically activated the rear wheel parking brakes.

This is a 1936 Hudson Custom Six Four-Door Sedan. Mom looks eager to get going if Junior will just get off the running board. The rocket shaped projectile hood ornament was made of red plastic and must be one of the earliest examples of rocketship influence on car design.

The Hudson front compartment was un-likely to be mistaken for any other car in 1936. Note the wide windshield, the electric hand control mounted on the steering column, the center-mounted instruments and controls, and the speedometer curved to match the curve of the dashboard. Hudson was the first American car builder to replace ammeter and oil pressure gauges with warning lights. The controls and dial for the built in radio are directly below the speedometer.

This view of a 1936 DeLuxe Straight-Eight Convertible Coupe shows the wide new windshield. The emblems on the front of the front fenders identify this car as an eight-cylinder, which was available with as much as 124 horsepower. This model had a 120-inch wheelbase.

Hudson entered more than just speed competitions. Driven by Wilbur Shaw (on the left), this 1936 DeLuxe Eight sedan had just won a trophy in the Gilmore Yosemite Economy run, a popular economy competition run in California. Earle Gilmore, president of the Gilmore Oil Co., is handing over the silver cup. Shaw and the Hudson had achieved 22.8 miles per gallon. Note that the Hudson dealer is Earle C. Anthony, the best-known Packard dealer in California.

SIR MALCOLM CAMPBELL AND 1936 HUDSON

The gentleman posing by this 127-inch wheelbase 1936 Hudson DeLuxe Eight is Sir Malcolm Campbell, then holder of the world land speed record. Campbell set the land speed record of 300 miles per hour in a specially built racing car, but he had also set seven speed records in February 1935 driving stock Hudsons, including 88.207 miles per hour for the flying mile.

For 1937, Hudson restyled the grille. Frames were redesigned and wheelbases lengthened slightly. Note that this car has right hand drive; it is a Custom Eight sedan built for export. Hudson sold well in Great Britain during the 1930s. Hudson built 19,848 cars in 1937 plus 83,436 Terraplanes.

This is a Custom Eight Victoria Coupe containing another Hudson innovation for 1937. A one-person sideways-facing seat was now available behind the front seat. With three passengers sitting in the wide front seat, Hudson claimed that this made it a four-passenger coupe. Bumpers have not yet been installed on this car.

1937 HUDSON

This view from the 1937 Hudson sales catalog shows a Custom Touring sedan on the 122-inch wheelbase. This model was available with either the 101-horsepower six (107 horsepower optional) or the 122-horsepower eight. Hudson added a vacuum-powered automatic clutch so that the Electric Hand could now be shifted without even declutching, simply by releasing the gas pedal. Hudson called this feature "Selective Automatic Shift" and nothing like it was yet available on any competitive cars.

Another view from the 1937 sales catalog shows an airbrush rendering of a car set against a photographic background. This is the top-of-the-line Custom Eight Sedan built on a 129-inch wheelbase and available only as an eight. Compare the wider front doors on this model with the 122-inch wheelbase sedan on the previous page.

Another Hudson innovation for 1937 was the introduction of the Convertible Brougham, shown in the lower photo. It was one of the first convertible club coupes with the rear seat brought inside the car. The car in the upper photo is a Custom Convertible Coupe without a full back seat, which continued to be available.

This Hudson Custom Six sedan has rare factory fender skirts. For 1938, the wheelbase on all Hudson Custom and DeLuxe Six and Eights was 122 inches, except for the Custom Country Club Eight, which was 129 inches.

For 1938, big Hudsons got a new grille with lots of horizontal chrome bars, and oval headlamps. This is a Custom Six Touring Sedan with a 212-cubic-inch engine and 101 horsepower, 107 horsepower optional.

Mr. P. W. Faust, a Hudson owner since 1912, is shown here taking delivery of his new 1938 Hudson Custom Eight Sedan at the factory. That's Mrs. Faust at the wheel. The Terraplane was also continued in 1938, but as part of the Hudson line, not as a separate marque. The Hudson Terraplane grille was similar to the Hudson, but had painted ribs instead of chrome, and round headlamps.

The Depression returned for a last act in 1938 and sales were down, so Hudson introduced a shorter, lower-priced model mid-year. The Hudson 112 (DeLuxe Sedan shown here) had a 112-inch wheelbase and was powered by a smaller version of the Hudson Six with 175 cubic inches and 83 horsepower. In spite of the new model, Hudson shipments for 1938 dropped to 51,078 cars.

The Hudson 112 Brougham (two-door sedan) became Hudson's lowest price sedan for 1938. In standard form, it sold for $724 and the DeLuxe model cost only $10 more!

In addition to supplying a Hudson convertible as pace car for the Indianapolis 500, Hudson supplied a fleet of Model 112 sedans for use by race officials. Seen here is Chester Ricker, official AAA timing director for the Indy 500. Hudson also sent a Model 112 to Bonneville, where it established several Class D records, including 80.50 miles per hour for 1 hour, and 70.58 miles per hour for 12 days and 20,327 miles.

Most 1939 Hudson models sported radically changed and streamlined front ends. On all but the One-twelve, the headlights were now flush-mounted in the fenders. The center grille was lower and flanked with catwalk side grilles. Two fashionably turned-out ladies are admiring the top-of-the-line Country Club Custom Sedan. Those are parking lights on the side of the hood.

The new grille ensemble blended well with the Hudson body design. This is a Hudson Six Coupe with a wheel-base of 118 inches and a 96-horsepower 212-cubic-inch engine.

The rear contours of the fastback sedans were rounded to provide more trunk room. This made the "Touring" body, or trunk back, alternative unnecessary, even though it was still available on some models. Note the high-mounted taillights, and the latest thing in women's shoes!

This is Hudson's top-of-the-line sedan for 1939, the Country Club Custom Sedan. The wheelbase was an extra long 129 inches and it was available only with the 122-horsepower 254-cubic-inch eight-cylinder engine.

This snappy looking coupe being admired by these two well-dressed women is a 1939 DeLuxe Six with a 118-inch wheelbase and a 212-cubic-inch 96-horsepower six-cylinder engine. All Hudsons were equipped with a steering column-mounted gearshift and a forward tipping (rear opening) hood this year.

The 1939 Hudson Country Club Convertible Brougham rode a 122-inch wheelbase and was available with either a 101-horsepower Six or a 122-horsepower Eight. This one has optional fender-mounted spare wheels. Note the unusual rear quarter window that lowered with the top. Hudson convertible club coupes were among the first convertibles to provide windows for rear seat passengers.

Hudson's lowest priced model was again the One-Twelve line, here seen displayed in touring sedan form. Wheelbase was 112 inches and the engine was a 175-cubic-inch 86-horsepower version of the Hudson Six. Notice the elegant furniture, oriental carpets, and grandfather clock in this showroom.

Hudson's lowest priced passenger car in 1939 was this Model One-Twelve Utility Coach with a price of $725. The car seated six, but the seats could be removed for cargo. In 1939, the One-Twelve models were the only Hudsons that did not have the headlights mounted in the fenders.

To pep up sales in mid-year, Hudson introduced the Pacemaker line in March 1939. This was a lower priced edition of the DeLuxe Six and used the same 118-inch wheelbase and 212-cubic-inch 96-horsepower engine. The Terraplane had been dropped, and some viewed the Pacemaker as the replacement. For 1939, Hudson shipments rose to 82,161 cars.

The Country Club interiors reached new heights of luxury for cars in Hudson's price range. This sumptuous rear compartment was trimmed in two-tone brown and tan Hockanum wool "accented with chrome." In 1940, this was Hudson's most luxurious model and the 125-inch wheelbase provided more rear seat legroom than other Hudsons.

The Hudson grille design was extensively changed again for 1940. The center vertical grill was completely gone; in its place were two low, horizontal air intakes decorated with seven horizontal chrome bars on each side. This car is a Country Club sedan now riding a slightly shortened 125-inch wheelbase and available with either a six- or eight-cylinder engine.

The middle-sized Hudsons for 1940 were the Super Six and Eight built on a 118-inch wheelbase. This is a Super Six Four-Door Touring Sedan displayed on a turntable on the roof of the Hudson factory in Detroit. The 212-cubic-inch Six now produced 102 horsepower.

Hudson offered several convertibles in 1940. Shown here is a Hudson Eight Convertible Club Coupe on a 118-inch wheelbase. The 254-cubic-inch eight-cylinder engine now developed 128 horsepower. All Hudsons were equipped with independent front suspension for 1940, and could be ordered with or without running boards.

Hudson was a pioneer of so-called "safety" hood design that could not catch the wind and open accidentally if left unlatched. It was locked with a lever inside the car. It looks like engine accessibility on this Hudson Six DeLuxe could be better, however.

For 1940, the lowest priced and smallest Hudson models were the Six Deluxe, seen here, and the Traveler Six, which was even cheaper. Both rode a 113-inch wheelbase and were powered by a smaller 175-cubic-inch version of the Hudson Six developing 92 horsepower. This Six DeLuxe Club Coupe could be had with either three or four passenger seating.

These women are admiring a 1940 Hudson Six DeLuxe Touring Sedan. Overdrive was available on all Hudsons for the first time and replaced Selective Automatic Shift, which was discontinued although an automatic clutch was still optional. Hudson shipped 86,865 cars for the 1940 model year, up slightly from 1939.

The 1941 Hudson grille looked similar to its predecessor, but now had nine cross bars instead of seven. Wheelbases were extended 3 inches on most models. This is a Commodore Eight, a new name replacing the Country Club designation for Hudson's top models.

Hudson's smallest sedan for 1941, the Six DeLuxe, now used a 116-inch wheelbase. A plainer version called the Traveler was also available. All 1941 Hudson sedan bodies were now indented at the rear belt line, replacing the fastback look with what is commonly called a "notchback." Two-tone paint schemes were popular in 1941.

Here is a 1941 Hudson Six DeLuxe Club Coupe, also available as a business coupe. Both the Six DeLuxe and Traveler models were powered by the 175-cubic-inch version of the Hudson six developing 92 horsepower. All Hudsons could be ordered with overdrive and/or an automatic clutch, which Hudson now called "Vacumotive Drive."

Hudson's middle market entry was the Super Six, seen here in Touring Sedan form. This model shared a longer 121-inch wheelbase with the new Commodore series. The 1941 Super Six used the 212-cubic-inch engine rated at 102 horsepower, which it also shared with the Commodore Six. All Hudsons used the same body shell regardless of wheelbase.

These women look ready for spring with this sharp 1941 Hudson Commodore Eight Convertible. The wheelbase was 121 inches and the eight-cylinder engine developed 128 horsepower. For 1941, Hudson shipped 79,529 cars.

This is the finest Hudson sedan for 1941, a Commodore Custom Four-Door Touring Sedan. It was built on its own exclusive 129-inch wheelbase chassis and was available only as an eight. The body was stretched by using the wider front doors from two-door models.

Making a rare appearance in the Hudson model line was this long and handsome station wagon. It was built on the Super Six 121-inch-wheelbase chassis and had seats for eight passengers, which could be removed. Unlike most car companies that offered wood body station wagons, Hudson built its own wooden bodies. The list price was $1,383, which made it the second highest priced Hudson in 1941.

For 1942, Hudson made few mechanical changes, but lots of styling changes: more chrome, skirted rear fenders, a wider grille, and concealed running boards. This is one of Hudson's lowest priced cars, a Six DeLuxe Club Sedan. The wheelbase was unchanged at 116 inches, as was power at 92 horsepower.

1942 HUDSON SUPER 6 COUPE

H·6900·56·CH

The next step up was the 1942 Hudson Super Six, also mechanically unchanged with a 121-inch wheelbase and a 212-cubic-inch 102-horsepower engine. This is a Club Coupe. Hudson offered a new semi-automatic transmission this year called "Drive-Master." It utilized technology from the Electric Hand days combined with the Vacumotive automatic clutch to permit shifting by releasing the accelerator pedal. It could be switched off (and often was) if it got out of adjustment.

Here is a Super Six Convertible Sedan ready for some fun in the sun. However, war clouds were gathering and car production would soon be shut down for several years. All Hudson convertibles were now equipped with power tops.

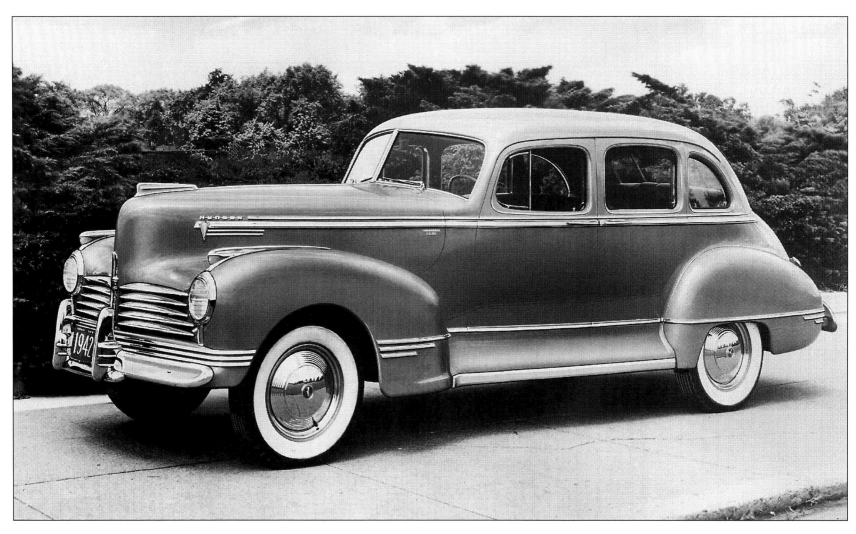

The extra chrome tells us this is the up-scale Commodore, in this case, an eight-cylinder touring sedan. Notice the fender-mounted parking lights and the huge hubcaps. Wheelbase was 121 inches and the engine was good for 128 horsepower. During the abbreviated 1942 production year, cut short by U.S. entry into World War II, Hudson built 40,661 cars.

Hudson continued the lavishly trimmed, extra sized Commodore Custom sedan for one last year. On a 128-inch wheelbase, this was luxurious transportation. The United States entered World War II on December 8, 1941, and civilian automobile production was shut down by February 1942.

Soon after World War II ended, production of Hudsons resumed on August 30, 1945. Few changes were noticeable from the 1942 models, but the most evident was the now recessed center section of the 1946 grille. The lower priced 116-inch wheelbase cars were dropped, as were the expensive Commodore Custom models. Left were Super and Commodore Sixes and Eights, all on the 121-inch wheelbase. New cars were in short supply in 1946 and this happy couple no doubt cannot believe their good fortune at getting a new Hudson Commodore Eight sedan.

The six and eight Commodores were identical, except of course for the engines, and were mechanically identical with the Supers. This 1946 Hudson Commodore Six sedan sported black sidewall tires because white sidewalls would not be available until 1947 at the earliest. All of the pre-war options were continued, including Drive-Master semi-automatic transmission.

Convertible production was resumed as soon as possible, and contributed to a near record model year production of 95,000 units for both 1946 and 1947. This is a 1946 Super Six Convertible. Commodore convertibles came only as eights. Could these sales rates be maintained? Hudson's greatest years were just ahead. The step-down was coming!

First encounters with the new 1948 Hudson step-down could be startling. The great width of the windshield and front fenders emphasized the low build of the car. The roof was 6 inches lower than contemporary Buicks and Chryslers. This Commodore sedan was photographed in April 1948 at the Hudson proving grounds.

This 1948 Commodore sedan view dates from April 1948, also at the proving grounds. The deeply curved windshield and tapering rear quarters accentuated the racy, streamlined look. Because the floors were recessed below the top of the side frame rails, the new Hudson soon became known by its advertising slogan, "The only car you step down into."

This X-ray view shows the unique and very robust body construction of the new step-down. Note that there were two sets of longitudinal frame rails with one set passing *outside* the rear wheels. The rear wheels could be accessed sufficiently for removal when the car was lifted by a body or bumper jack. The welded unit body/frame incorporated built in jack pads for safer jacking. Hudson called its method of body building "Monobilt."

The vast width of the seats in a step-down is shown in this view of the rear compartment of a Commodore four-door, Hudson's top-of-the-line sedan. The floor was several inches below the doorsill, a first for any American car builder. Commodore window moldings were finished in a blond wood grain pattern. Because the rear seat was located entirely ahead of the rear wheel housings, it was 63 inches wide, the widest in the industry at the time. The recessed door panels, another Hudson innovation, provided additional interior width.

This profile view at the proving grounds shows the streamlined taper of the rear of the car, and the slim side windows. The 1948 and 1949 models were often seen with a subtly shaded two-tone paint scheme, as demonstrated by this Commodore sedan. The area below the side character crease line was painted a lighter shade of the upper body color. All 1948 and 1949 Hudsons were built on a 124-inch wheelbase. Model year production for 1948 rose to 117,200 cars.

Two women admire a new 1948 Hudson; in this case, a Commodore Six club coupe. The setting was the roof of one of the Hudson factory buildings in Detroit, walled off so that prying eyes of competitors could not see from nearby buildings what Hudson was up to. Hudson introduced a brand new inline six-cylinder engine to power the revolutionary new cars. It was a 262-cubic-inch L-head design, and at the time, was the largest and most powerful six-cylinder engine offered in any American production car. It was the first Hudson engine to provide full pressure lubrication. It was also larger and more powerful than the Hudson straight-eight, which was continued as an option.

Although shown in sales catalogs from the introduction of the step-down, the convertible was not put into production until August 1948, near the end of the 1948 model year. However, the 1949 models were virtually identical. These Hudson convertibles were very roomy, and very sturdy because of the unit construction body.

This shows the dashboard of a 1949 Commodore convertible and was typical of all 1948 and 1949 Commodores. Note the centered dials and two glove compartments. The large reinforced windshield header contained sun visors, a map light, and swiveling radio antenna, and was unique to Hudson convertibles.

The step-down was a hit! Hudson executives gathered to celebrate the 40th anniversary of the Hudson Motor Car Company in April 1949. The old car is a 1909 Hudson Model 20 and the new one is a 1949 Commodore convertible with Hudson President A. E. Barit at the wheel. Model year production reached 159,100 cars, Hudson's best year since 1929.

The rear of a step-down was especially sleek, as shown by this 1949 Super series. The fancier Commodores had larger taillights and more decoration. In the background are a 1949 model to the right and a 1950 Hudson to the left, illustrating the changes in the grille design made to the 1950 models.

For 1950, the step-down got its first facelift. One cross bar was removed from the grille, and two vertical bars inserted near the center, to suggest a triangle shape. The Hudson logo had long been a white triangle. The car shown is a Pacemaker, a low cost addition to the Hudson lineup for 1950.

In addition to the revised grille, 1950 Commodores added a rub rail midway between the rocker panels and the crease line stamped in the side sheet metal. Sedan rear windows were also enlarged. Hudson offered a unique semi-automatic transmission in 1950 called Super-matic. With the twist of a switch, the driver could select manual shifting, clutchless shifting, or semi-automatic shifting with overdrive.

Hudson expanded its model line in 1950 with the addition of the Pacemaker series, shown here. The step-down body was mounted on a shorter wheelbase (119 inches instead of 124 inches) with a destroked version of the new six (232 cubic inches instead of 262 cubic inches) and very spartan interior trim. The result was a price of $1,933 for the cheapest Pacemaker sedan, $349 less than a Commodore Six sedan. The Pacemaker was available in sedan form as shown here, as well as two-door, club coupe, and convertible.

This 1950 Custom Commodore Eight convertible shows off the new side trim, as well as its ability to attract ad-mirers. The Commodore Eight Convertible Brougham sold 426 copies for the year, while total Hudson convertible production for the year, all series, reached an impressive 4,115 units. Total 1950 model year production of all body types reached 121,408 cars.

For 1951, major changes were made to the Hudson grille. Horizontal bars were fewer and bolder, and curved gracefully down to the parking lights. This is a Hornet, an exciting addition to the Hudson line. Powered by an enlarged version of Hudson's new six, the Hornet, with its low center of gravity and superior handling, soon became king of the stock car tracks. With 308 cubic inch displacement, the Hornet Six was larger than many eight-cylinder engines then on the market.

The new Hornet carried the same trim and upholstery as the Commodore series. The Hornet series was distinguished by a gold plated triangle on the hood ornament, large chrome "Hornet" badges on the sides of the front fenders and on the trunk, additional badges inside, and, of course, the powerful new engine.

This Commodore Custom six-cylinder was no performance slouch either. All Hudsons shared the superior road-ability and handling of the step-down body. Another change for 1951 was a revamped dashboard with gauges and controls moved to positions in front of the driver. General Motors' Hydra-Matic automatic transmission became available as an option on Commodores and Hornets.

With production of 34,495 cars for 1951, the Pacemaker series had become an important part of the Hudson line. The photo shows a Pacemaker Custom sedan. Total production of all Hudsons for the 1951 model year reached 131,915 cars, of which 43,666 were the new Hornet series.

In 1952, the step-down was entering its fifth production year and so more facelifting was done to freshen up appearances. Bright trim was added around the windows to give sedans and coupes the look of hardtops. The rub rail was made heavier and raised to the crease line stamped into the doors and fenders. Shown is a Hornet club coupe, still clean and fast looking in spite of the added brightwork.

The 1952 Hudson model lineup was shuffled somewhat. The Super Six was dropped, and the 262-cubic-inch engine and trim were transferred to the shorter 119-inch wheelbase Pacemaker platform. The result was named the "Wasp," and it was marketed as a junior edition of the Hornet. The Pacemaker continued with its smaller engine and plain trim. Shown is a Wasp four-door sedan. Model year production fell to 70,000 cars.

Hudson was a bit late to the "hard-top" parade. A hardtop was a coupe body style that used convertible-type windows and became popular starting in 1950. The step-down body design did not lend itself to modification, but Hudson managed to come up with a hardtop, presumably based on the Hudson convertible. Hudson named its version the "Hollywood," and it was introduced late in the 1951 model year. The car shown is a 1952 Wasp Hollywood. Note the absence of a "B" pillar with the windows lowered.

Hudson still offered a good selection of convertibles in 1952. Four distinct models were available: Hornet, Commodore Eight, Commodore Six, and Wasp. Tops made of a new synthetic fiber called Orlon were available at extra cost, as shown on this Wasp convertible.

Hudson sales were dropping, and funds to do a major redesign of the step-down were lacking, so only minor changes were made for 1953. The two vertical grille bars were removed and the hood ornament was changed to simulate an air scoop. This is a Hornet, with a tired 1949 Commodore in the background. The 1953 model line was reduced: the Commodore Six and Eight series were both dropped and the Pacemaker became the Wasp. What had been the Wasp in 1952 became the Super Wasp.

Entering its sixth year of production, the step-down was little changed, yet looked as sleek and swift as it ever had. This is a 1953 Hornet sedan. Unfortunately, the American motoring public was being conditioned by the major car builders to demand big changes every year, and so Hudson sales were suffering. Despite the clean lines and enviable stock car racing record, sales of big Hudsons dropped from a high of 159,100 for the 1949 model year to 45,000 in 1953.

Upholstery fabrics and patterns were changed for 1953. This Hornet sedan interior shows a check weave nylon fabric available in a choice of colors. Even genuine leather was available in closed as well as open models by special order.

It was still a commodious and luxurious rear compartment, replete with amenities. Notice the extra wide center armrest, the reading lamps, the assist straps by the vent window, the ash receiver, map pocket, and robe cord on the back of the front seat. In addition, extra foot room was afforded by the step-down design.

The previous year's Wasp became the Super Wasp in 1953. With a 262-cubic-inch engine in the short 119-inch-wheelbase chassis, this car could run with the Hornets.

The trunk of the step-down, although limited in height, was actually quite roomy because it was so deep.

Here is the rear of the step-down in its cleanest form. This 1953 Hornet sedan carried the Hudson badges of power. The Hornet emblem told the world that under the hood was the power of the stock car champion. The Twin H Power badge indicated that the car was equipped with a dual carburetor intake manifold and probably had a high-compression cylinder head that would be good for 160 horsepower with a top speed of over 100 miles per hour. If you were passed by this in 1953, it was probably futile to pursue.

This is the face of Hudson's 20 million dollar folly, the Jet. Introduced in November 1952 to meet a small car market that wouldn't materialize for another five years, the Jet was the wrong car at the wrong time. Money spent to design and tool the Jet could have been better spent redesigning the step-down and designing a modern overhead-valve V8 engine.

Although the 1953 Jet was constructed like its big brother the step-down, it came out tall and narrow instead of low and wide. Thus, it did not have the roadability or sleek lines of the senior Hudsons. Yet, it was well built, space efficient, and economical.

Frank Spring, Hudson's capable chief designer, was very disappointed in the appearance of the production Jet. The 1952 Ford apparently became a role model, thanks to influential Hudson dealer Jim Moran and Hudson president A. E. Barit, who advocated the raised fender line, wraparound rear window, chair high seats (and high roof), and round taillights. Unfortunately, not many found the resulting proportions attractive. This is a Super Jet sedan, the deluxe version. Hudson Jet sales were 21,143 cars for the 1953 model year.

The handsome dash of a Super Jet featured a large steering wheel. Jets were available with Hydra-Matic, overdrive, or manual three-speed transmissions in two- and four-door body types. There were no convertibles, hardtops, or station wagons, although a utility version of the two-door with a removable rear seat became available in the second year of production.

The engine compartment of the Jet bore a definite Hudson family resemblance. The Jet engine was an inline L-head six like the Hornet, and a Hudson "Twin H Power" dual carburetor intake manifold was an option, as was a high-compression head. With both options, the Jet generated 114 horsepower and was a very peppy performer. Displacement was 202 cubic inches.

The Hudson Italia was what would today be called a concept car. It was designed by Chief Hudson Designer Frank Spring and built by Italian coachbuilder Carrozzeria Touring of Milan. The Italia was announced August 25, 1953, and was Hudson's last look at future automotive design as an independent company.

Like many automotive designs in the early 1950s, the Italia showed some jet aircraft influences. The "jet exhaust tubes" actually housed the taillights. Power came from a 114-horsepower 202-cubic-inch Hudson Jet engine. On January 14, 1954, Hudson announced that the Italia would be produced in limited numbers, and eventually 25 more were built and sold.

The interior of the Italia was very roomy for such a sporty car, and offered many innovations, such as a wraparound windshield, and doors cut into the roof to afford easier access. Of course, step-down floors were included. The dash came from a Hudson Jet.

Entering its seventh year of production, the big Hudson finally received a major facelift. Unfortunately, it was difficult to "square off" the step-down or enlarge the glass area, both styling trends of the time. A one-piece windshield was used for the first time. The grille was simplified and the new hood now had a functional air scoop. Shown is a Hornet sedan.

New triangular shaped taillights were mounted high on the raised rear fenders and the trunk lid was squared off. New brightwork mounted below the rub rail suggested a rear fender contour, something the step-down had never had. Except for the one-piece windshield, glass area was unchanged.

This is the front compartment of a top-of-the-line Hornet sedan. The dash received a major redesign and power steering and power brakes were available for the first time. The 1954 models were introduced in October 1953. The big Hudsons continued the same model lineup as in 1953. Production of the big Hudsons (Hornets and Wasps) declined to 36,436 cars for 1954.

Upholstery was restyled and this was the most luxurious interior ever put into a step-down. The door armrests were now built-in, and the middle cushion in the backrest folded down as a wide center armrest. This is a Hornet interior: the Super Wasp and Wasp interiors were less plush.

This is a 1954 Hornet engine bay equipped with Twin H Power dual carburetors. In this form, with 7.5:1 high-compression head, Hornet power was now 170 horsepower. Single carburetor versions were good for 160 horsepower. Both power increases were due to improvements in the design of the combustion chamber to improve breathing, which Hudson called "Super Induction."

To boost lagging sales, a lower cost Hornet was introduced March 19, 1954. This was the Hornet Special, which used Super Wasp interiors and exterior trim on the longer 124-inch Hornet wheelbase with the 160-horsepower Hornet engine. This allowed a buyer to obtain a Hornet sedan for about $150 less. Body styles offered were a four-door, a club coupe, and for the first time on any Hornet, a two-door club sedan, as shown here. The last step-down built, and the last Hudson built in Detroit, came off the line October 29, 1954.

For 1954, the Jet was little changed. Two bright metal rub strips were added to the previously unadorned flanks of the Super Jet shown here. The ribs at the rear of the center grille bar were extended forward.

A deluxe third series was added to the Jet line to spur disappointing sales. The Jetliner was available as a two-
or four-door, and carried extra chrome trim on the rear fender or rear door. Jetliners were often equipped with
an outside spare tire carrier as shown here. This tire carrier was made an option for all Jets.

Rear seat legroom in the Jet was expanded slightly in 1954, as this photo is intended to demonstrate. This is a Jetliner, available in white vinyl with a choice of red, green, or blue bolsters and trim. In spite of the addition of the flashy Jetliner, Jet sales slumped from 21,143 for 1953 to 14,224 in 1954. Hudson was out of money, with no attractive new models ready, and in trouble.

This is a 1954 Jetliner two-door trying unsuccessfully to resemble a flashy hardtop. The Hudson Jetliner name preceded the actual introduction of jet-powered U.S. airliners by four years. It was apparent by early 1954 that Hudson's future was dim. The result was merger with Nash to form American Motors Corporation (AMC) on April 22, 1954.

After the AMC merger, Hudson production in Detroit was shut down except for engine manufacture. New 1955 Hudsons were built using Nash bodies and platforms. This was the new grille design for 1955, shown on a Wasp. The overall shape of the grille resembled earlier Hudsons, but not much else did.

The Hornets used the 121-inch wheelbase Nash Ambassador platform, which was 3 inches shorter than the step-down. This is the Hollywood Custom hardtop model. Unlike the Nash, the Hudson version did not use skirted wheels. Bright two-tone paint schemes were in fashion in 1955 and Hudson did its part.

Shown is a more sedately painted Hornet sedan. Most of the Custom trim Hornets were equipped with the outside spare tire carrier. The rugged and powerful 160-horsepower Hornet six continued to be the base engine, and a Packard-built 320-cubic-inch overhead-valve V-8 offering 208 horsepower was available.

This is a Wasp sedan for 1955, now built on the Nash Statesman 114-inch wheelbase platform, a reduction of 5 inches from the step-down version. The Wasp had lost some of its sting as well. The big 262-cubic-inch six was replaced with the much smaller 202-cubic-inch Jet six. It was a small engine to haul around such a large body.

Inside, there were a few reminders of the Hudson heritage. The Hudson instrument cluster and steering wheel from the 1954 models were used, as was the Hudson radio. However, it was a Nash dashboard with center-mounted pull-out glove drawer and the Nash Weather-Eye heating system.

The Nash body had seats as wide as the Hudson step-down, and a rear seat center armrest that was even wider. This is a 1955 Hudson Hornet Hollywood Custom with nylon and vinyl seat trim. The glass areas of the Nash body were considerably larger than the Hudson step-down and thus were more in keeping with the design trends of 1955. Hudsons now offered the familiar Nash features of reclining seats and convertible beds.

The 1955 Hudson Hornet was an attractive enough car in its own right, but it bore little resemblance to previous Hudsons in either appearance or roadability. Like the step-downs, the new car was built with unit-body construction. Nash had been a unit construction pioneer since 1941.

The stern of the 1955 Hudson, or "Hash" as some Hudson fans labeled it. Not much resemblance here to the sleek aerodynamic shape of the step-down. The floors were no longer "step-down" and so the height and center of gravity were higher. This is a Wasp with optional outside tire carrier.

For 1955, the Jet was dropped and Hudson dealers were given Ramblers to sell with Hudson grille badges. The Rambler was growing in popularity and offered a wider choice of models, so this was a beneficial arrangement. Ramblers sold by Hudson dealers received Hudson badging and hubcaps in 1955 and 1956. After that, they were just labeled Ramblers.

Sales of the Nash-based Hudson had dropped to 20,321 cars in 1955. The 1956 models were aggressively restyled to try to carve out a new market niche, since many traditional Hudson buyers had apparently been lost. An elaborate new grille and completely revised ornamentation were an attempt to straighten out the lines to match auto fashion trends of the time. This is a top-of-the-line Hornet Hollywood hardtop.

The new side trim on this 1956 Hornet V-8 sedan bore little relationship to the contours of the body panels. Unfortunately, 1956 was the year that three-tone color schemes made their appearance in the auto industry. As this car demonstrates, there had to be plenty of trim strips to separate all of the colors. The engine in this car was the overhead-valve V-8 supplied by Packard and increased in size to 352 cubic inches and 220 horsepower.

Taillights were changed for 1956, and small chrome fins were added. This is a Hornet Special sedan, a mid-year model addition. In its last year of production, the legendary L-head 308-cubic-inch Hornet six was still available, newly equipped with hydraulic valve lifters. The Nash body design restricted access for adjusting the Hornet six-cylinder engine side valves so that it was necessary to install self-adjusting tappets.

Here it is, the fanciest 1956 Hudson, a Hornet Hollywood Custom hardtop in all of its multi-hued glory. As if three different paint colors and all that chrome were not enough, the inset horizontal panel on the rear fender was covered with gold anodized aluminum. The newly added scoops over the headlights were non-functional. Buyers were not impressed with all of this glitter as only 1,053 of this Packard-powered model were sold.

This 1956 Hornet Custom sedan has the optional Packard supplied V-8. With a mere two paint colors and no continental tire carrier, this car looks much less gaudy. Tailfins began appearing on American cars in 1956 and Hudson joined the party with the modest chrome fins seen here.

On March 5, 1956, a new model was introduced. The Hornet Special used the shorter Wasp 114-inch wheelbase platform equipped with a new 250-cubic-inch 190-horsepower overhead-valve V-8 engine. This was the first V-8 built by American Motors and gave the new model very good performance. This is a Hornet Special Hollywood Custom.

This is the sedan version of the new Hornet Special. In spite of the new models, Hudson big car production fell to 10,671 cars for the 1956 model year, about half of the 1955 production.

For the 1957 model, Hudson designers again tinkered with the exterior trim. The roof panel was flattened and wheels were reduced in size from 15 inches to 14 inches to bring down the height. At the rear, the tacked on fins were enlarged, and the outside tire carrier became optional. In both photos, the 1957 model is the car on the right.

All Hudsons were now Hornets and built on the longer 121-inch wheelbase platform. The Wasp was dropped, as were all six-cylinder engines and the Packard-built V-8. All 1957 Hudsons used the new AMC V-8, enlarged to 327 cubic inches and developing 255 horsepower. This is a Hornet Custom four-door sedan.

This is the top-of-the-line, a 1957 Hudson Hornet Custom Hollywood hardtop. Models available were reduced to four: Custom sedan and hardtop and Super sedan and hardtop. Total production of Hudsons for the last year was only about 4,000 cars.

Here is a 1957 Hornet Super sedan, showing the enlarged, but still very "tacked on" tailfins. All Chrysler Corporation cars appeared with huge tailfins this year, and the competition had to try to keep up. The color insert on the front fender and door was painted on the Supers.

This is a Hornet Custom sedan. The anodized aluminum panel on the sides of the Custom models was moved from the rear fender to the front for 1957 and the color changed from gold to silver. About the only Hudson engineering feature that remained was the mechanical reserve on the brake pedal. If the hydraulic system failed, pushing on the brake pedal activated the rear brakes mechanically. It was an early version of the dual braking systems found on newer cars today.

The last vestiges of Hudson had disappeared from the dashboard as well. The Hudson radio and steering wheel were replaced by Nash designs. A new gauge cluster with a thermometer-style speedometer replaced the 1954 Hudson gauges, but at least it was unique to Hudsons and not used on Nashes. This is a 1957 Hornet Custom; the 1956 dashboard was similar.

A last look at the one of the last Hudson automobiles, a 1957 Hornet Custom Hollywood. The AMC V-8 gave the car powerful performance reminiscent of Hornets of old. Nevertheless, American Motors had made the decision to drop the Hudson and Nash cars and replace them with an enlarged version of the Rambler named Ambassador. The last Hudson was built at Kenosha, Wisconsin, on June 25, 1957, bringing to a close a memorable chapter in American automotive history.